Orchids of Nillumbik

(left) Purplish Beard-orchid and Red Beard-orchid (right)

First published by Busybird Publishing 2019

Copyright © 2019 Lydia Heap

ISBN 978-1-925949-50-6 (soft cover)
ISBN 978-1-925949-51-3 (hard cover)

Cover image: Wax-Lip Orchid

Back cover image: Wine-lip Spider-orchid

Cover design: Busybird Publishing

Layout and typesetting: Busybird Publishing

www.LydiaHeap.com

Busybird Publishing

2/118 Para Road
Montmorency, Victoria
Australia 3094
www.busybird.com.au

Notched Onion-orchid

Introduction

For years I have been photographing native orchids in Nillumbik, mostly around Panton Hill, Smiths Gully and Christmas Hills. Many people have noticed me as I am always barefoot in the bush to minimise damage.

This book is a showcase of some of the orchids from the area, it does not attempt to be a field guide or a scientific work. There are plenty of books and internet sites that give further details. It is simply an attempt to show people the wonderful flowers that can still be found near Melbourne.

Please look after any orchids you come across (in fact every part of the bush). Be careful when observing and photographing them. I always talk to my subjects and ask how they are going and if it's ok to photograph them, this seems to result in better photographs. No, I'm not mad, but talking to them creates a sense of empathy and enables you to capture their best features.

I often take people on orchid walks who say they have never seen any. It turns out that they have seen them but never noticed. Most Victorian orchids are small and cryptic, but once you tune into them, you will see more and more.

Large Duck Orchid

How to use this book

The orchids are roughly arranged in flowering order. Each has their peak flowering shown on the calendar in dark grey and possible flowering months in light grey. Although some individual plants may choose not to follow the accepted flowering months, I guess they have not read all the text books.

I have included other variations as often guides only contain one colour version of each orchid which can make identifying unusual ones hard (also it gives me an excuse for adding more photos).

Most of the photos in this book were taken with a compact FinePix S5800 camera from Fujifilm, and the only editing has been cropping and rotating. All the orchids are found on public land, some are quite rare and are in cages to protect them from wildlife and poachers.

The orchid species are constantly being reviewed so I have included synonyms where revisions are being undertaken. For further details on Victorian orchids I have found the web pages created by "RetiredAussies" and "VicFlora" to be most helpful.

Rosella Spider-orchid

Spring

The season that the bush seems to wake-up.

My record is 26 species in 3 hours; can you better that!

Salmon Sun-orchid

Crimson Spider-orchid

Arachnorchis concolor

Synonym: *Caladenia concolor*

J F M A M J J A **S** **O** N D

Flower size ≈ 8.0 cm   Plant height ≈ 30 cm

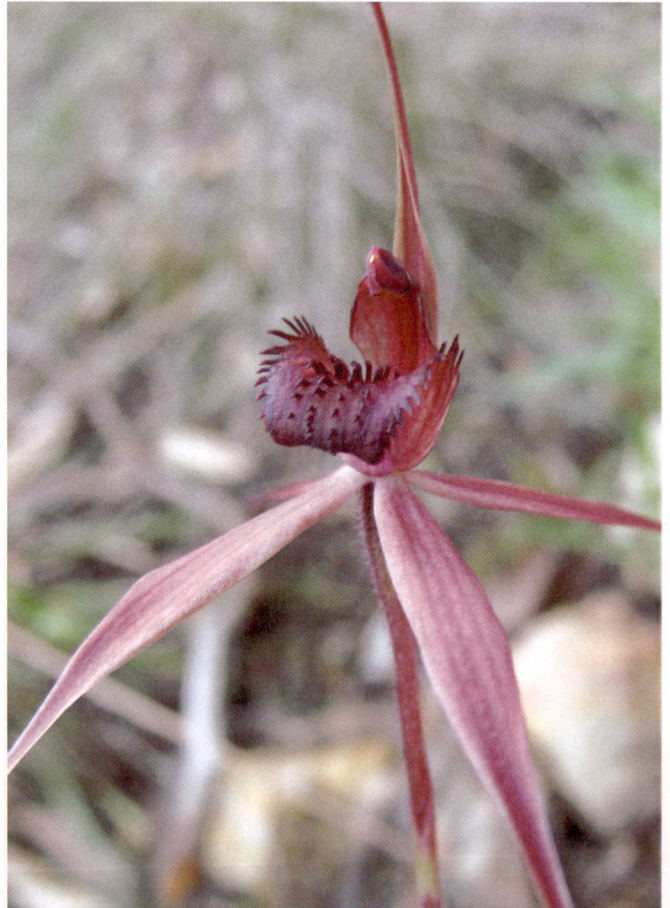

Crested Sun-orchid

Thelymitra ×irregularis

J F M A M J J A **S O** N D

Flower size ≈ 2.5 cm   Plant height ≈ 40 cm

Daddy Long-legs

Jonesiopsis filamentosa

Synonym: *Caladenia filamentosa*

J F M A M J J A S O N D

Flower size ≈ 7.0 cm   Plant height ≈ 45 cm

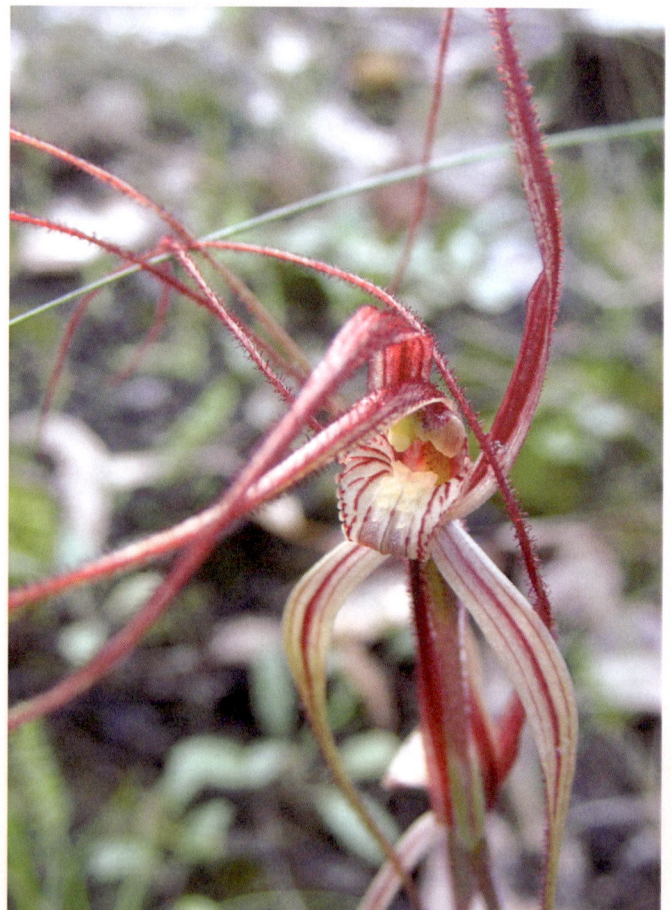

Tiny (Pygmy) Caladenia

Petalochilus pusillus

Synonym: *Caladenia pusilla*

J F M A M J J A **S** O **N** D

Flower size ≈ 1.2 cm   Plant height ≈ 10 cm

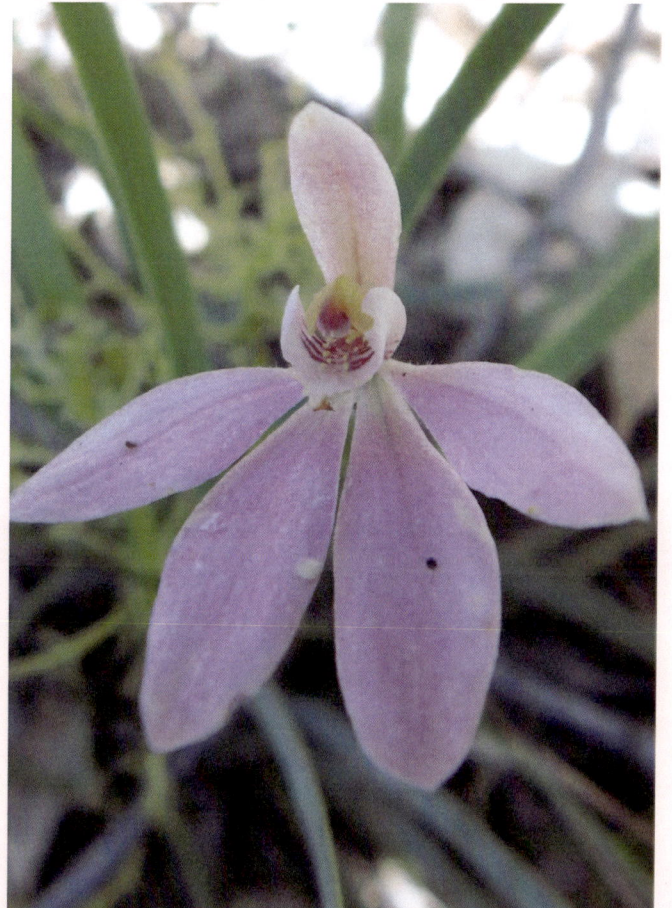

Slender Greenhood

Pterostylis foliata

J F M A M J J A S O N D

Flower size ≈ 2.5 cm   Plant height ≈ 30 cm

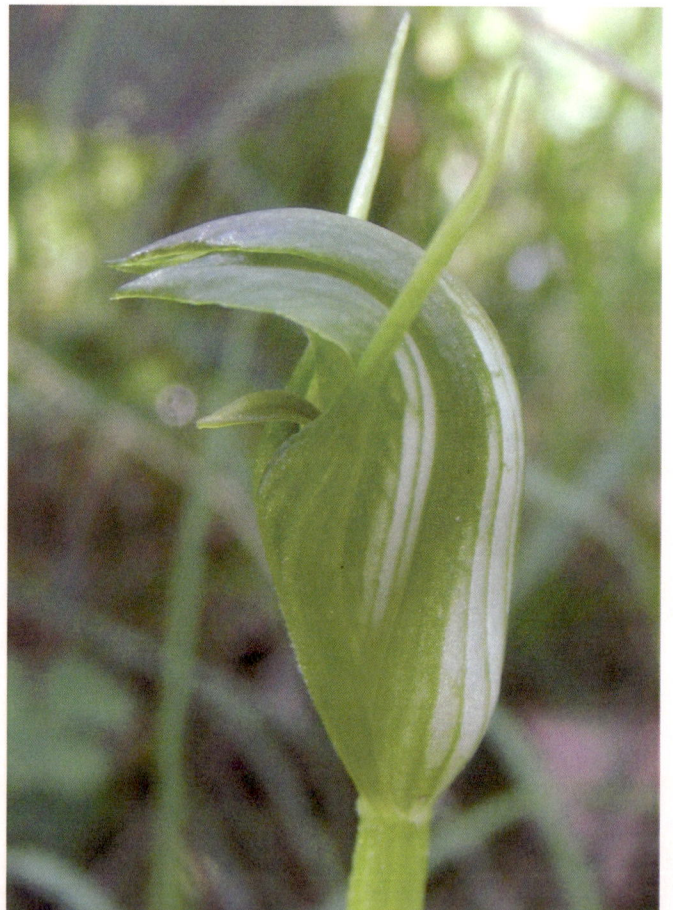

Golden Moths

Diuris chryseopsis

J F M A M J J A **S** **O** N D

Flower size ≈ 5.5 cm   Plant height ≈ 40 cm

Dusky Caladenia

Petalochilus fuscatus

Synonym: *Caladenia fuscata*

J F M A M J J A S O N D

Flower size ≈ 2.5 cm   Plant height ≈ 12 cm

Dusky Caladenia

White form

Plain-lip Spider-orchid

Arachnorchis clavigera

Synonym: *Caladenia clavigera*

J	F	M	A	M	J	J	A	S	O	N	D

Flower size ≈ 4.0 cm   Plant height ≈ 40 cm

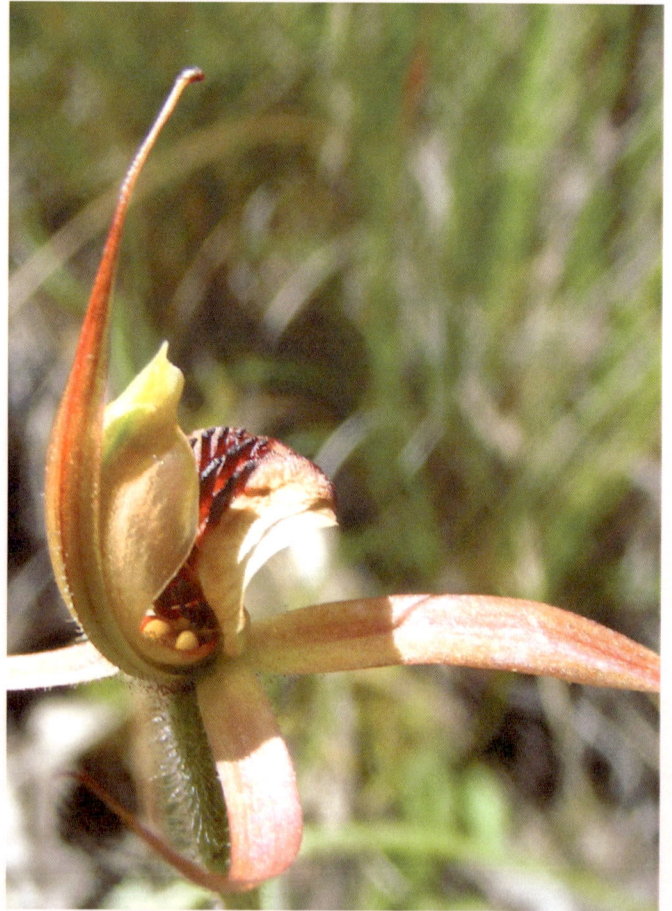

Alpine Greenhood

Pterostylis alpina

J F M A M J J A **S O** N D

Flower size ≈ 3.0 cm   Plant height ≈ 30 cm

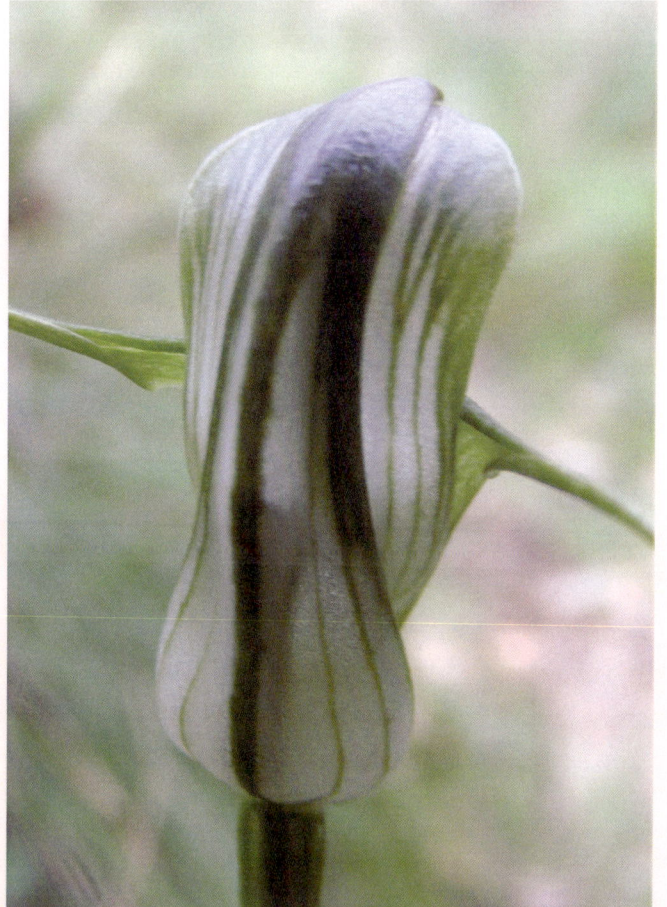

Pink Fingers

Petalochilus carneus

Synonym: *Caladenia carnea*

J F M A M J J A S O N D

Flower size ≈ 3.0 cm   Plant height ≈ 25 cm

Pink Fingers

Pale form

Sharp Greenhood

Pterostylis ×ingens

J F M A M J J A **S** O **N** D

Flower size ≈ 3.5 cm   Plant height ≈ 50 cm

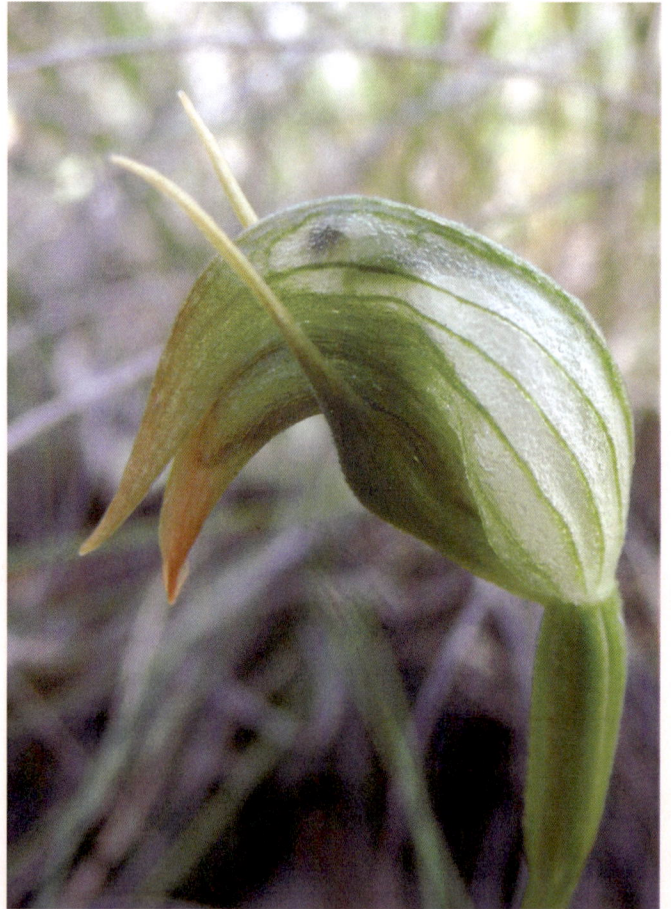

Hare Orchid

Leptoceras menziesii

J F M A M J J A **S O** N D

Flower size ≈ 1.5 cm   Plant height ≈ 25 cm

Purplish Beard-orchid

Calochilus robertsonii

J F M A M J J A S O N D

Flower size ≈ 3.0 cm   Plant height ≈ 45 cm

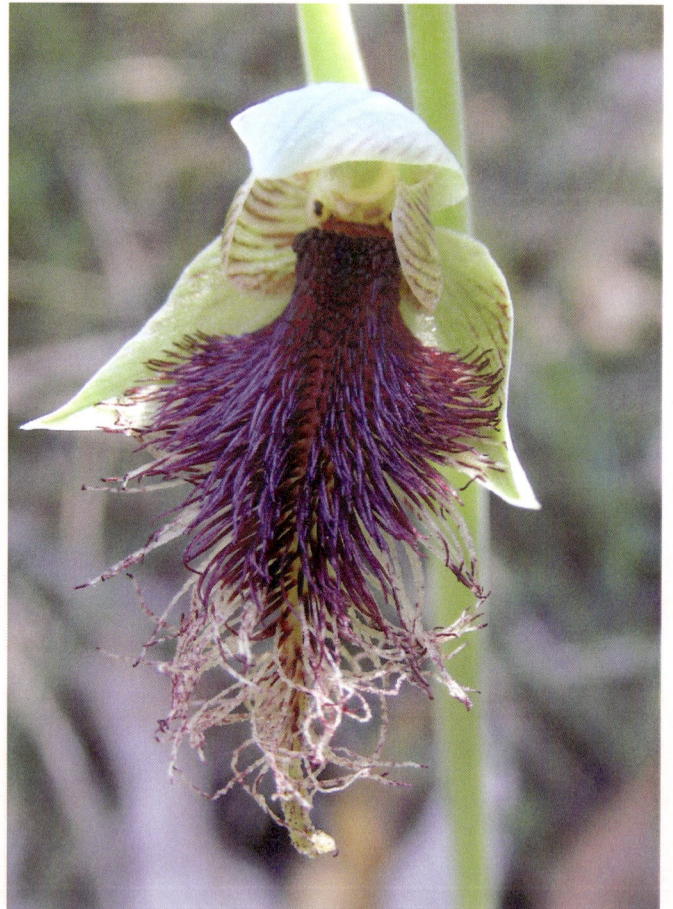

Pink Sun-orchid

Thelymitra carnea

J F M A M J J A S O N D

Flower size ≈ 1.5 cm   Plant height ≈ 20 cm

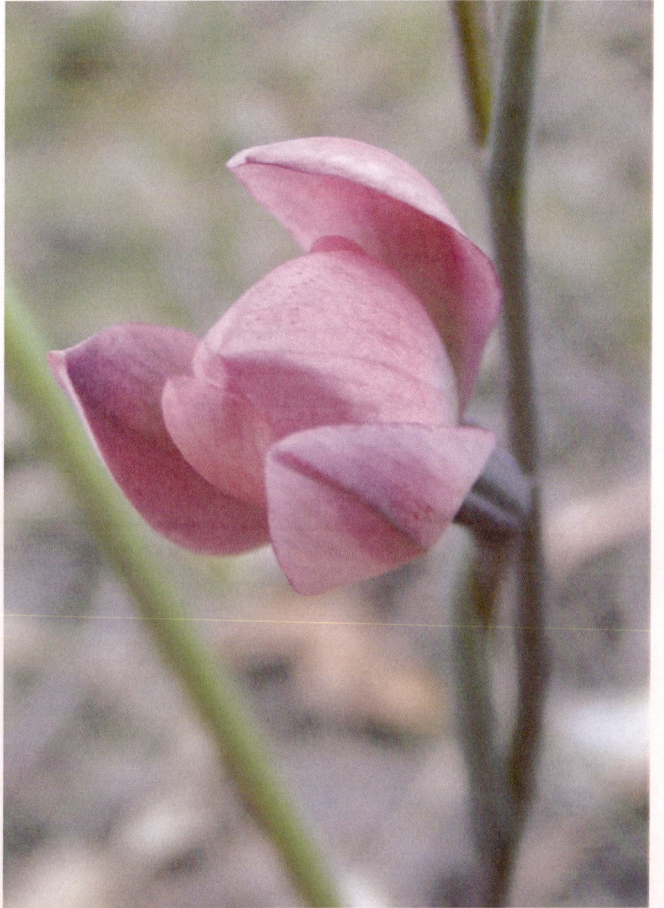

Wax-lip Orchid

Glossodia major

J F M A M J J A S O N D

Flower size ≈ 4.5 cm   Plant height ≈ 30 cm

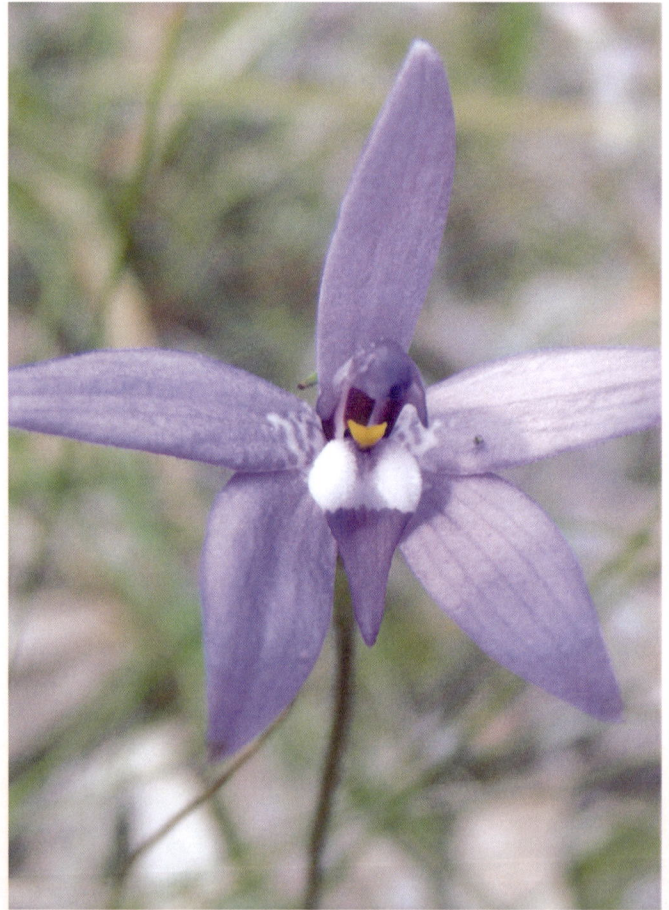

Wax-lip Orchid

Pale form

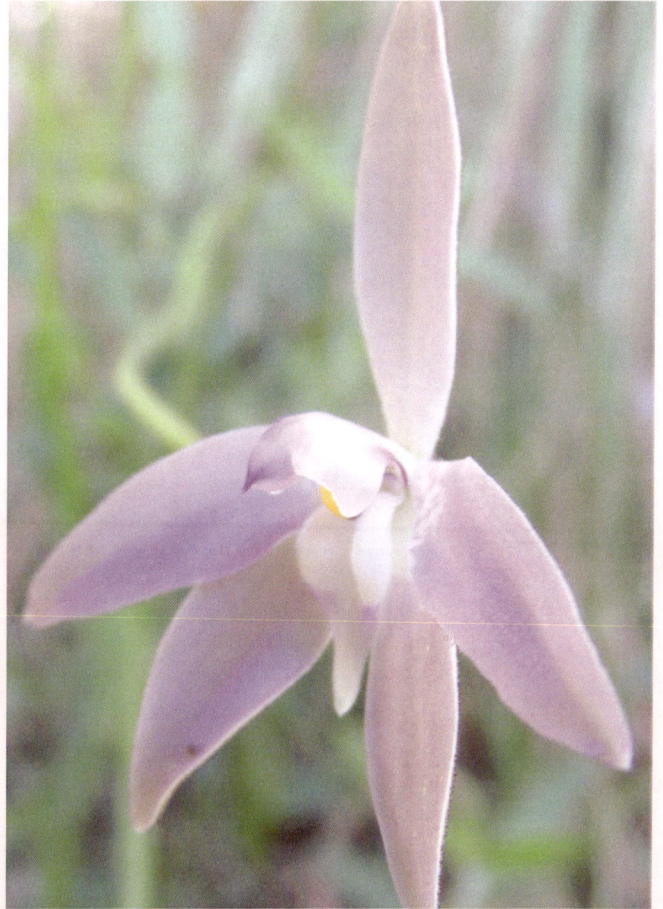

Spotted Sun-orchid

Thelymitra ixioides

| J | F | M | A | M | J | J | A | S | O | N | D |

Flower size ≈ 3.5 cm   Plant height ≈ 60 cm

Red Beard-orchid

Calochilus paludosus

J F M A M J J A **S O N** D

Flower size ≈ 2.5 cm   Plant height ≈ 35 cm

Green-comb Spider-orchid

Arachnorchis parva

Synonym: *Caladenia parva*

J	F	M	A	M	J	J	A	S	O	N	D

Flower size ≈ 4.0 cm   Plant height ≈ 25 cm

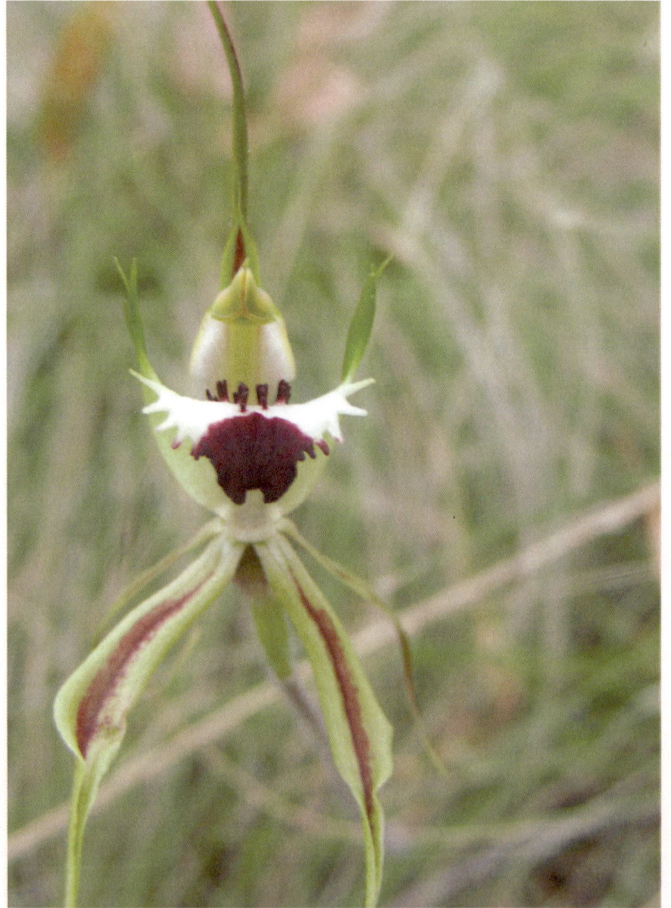

Green-comb Spider-orchid

Double headed and colour variations

Musky Caladenia

Stegostyla moschata

Synonym: *Caladenia moschata*

J F M A M J J A S O N D

Flower size ≈ 4.0 cm   Plant height ≈ 45 cm

Slender Onion-orchid

Microtis parviflora

| J | F | M | A | M | J | J | A | S | O | N | D |

Flower size ≈ 0.3 cm   Plant height ≈ 50 cm

Tiger Orchid

Diuris sulphurea

| J | F | M | A | M | J | J | A | S | O | N | D |

Flower size ≈ 3.0 cm   Plant height ≈ 50 cm

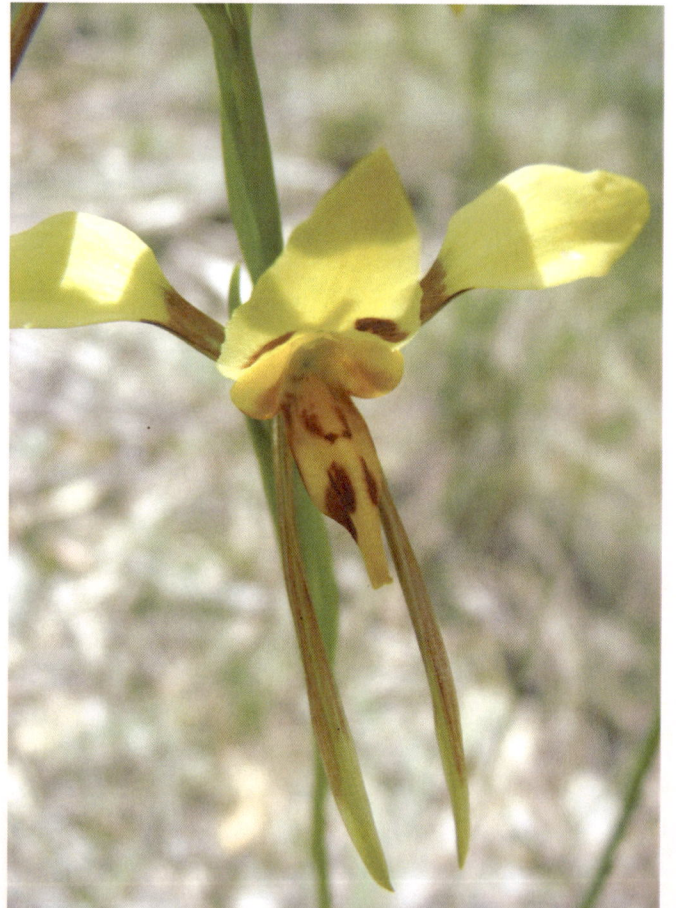

Tiger Orchid

Unmarked form

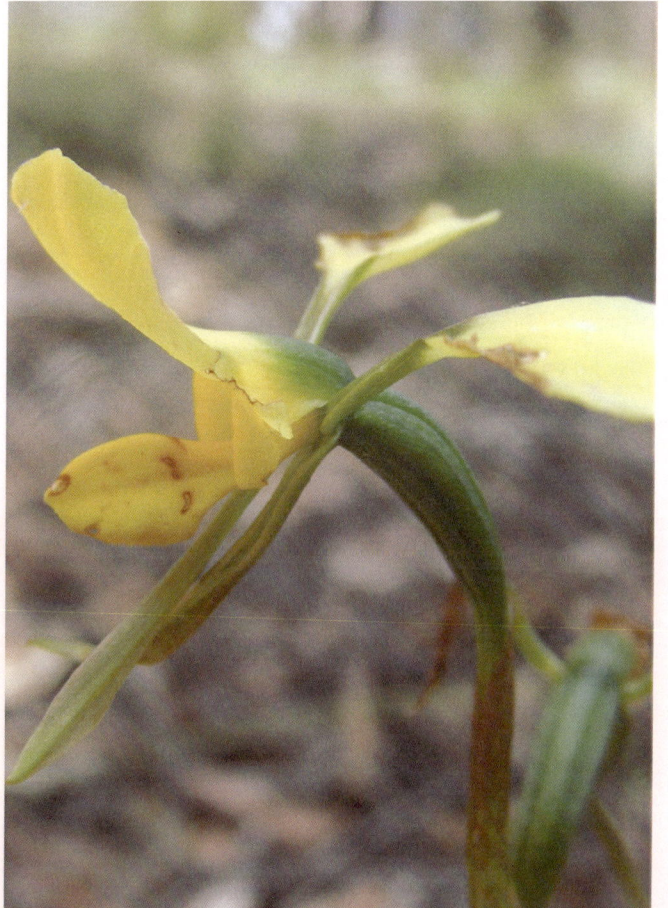

Slender Sun-orchid

Thelymitra pauciflora

J	F	M	A	M	J	J	A	S	O	N	D

Flower size ≈ 2.0 cm   Plant height ≈ 50 cm

Large Duck Orchid

Caleana major

J F M A M J J A S **O N** D

Flower size ≈ 4.5 cm   Plant height ≈ 30 cm

Common Bird-orchid

Chiloglottis valida

J	F	M	A	M	J	J	A	S	O	N	D

Flower size ≈ 4.0 cm   Plant height ≈ 6 cm

Common Bird-orchid

Green form

Wallflower Orchid

Diuris orientis

J F M A M J J A S **O** N D

Flower size ≈ 5.0 cm   Plant height ≈ 45 cm

Notched Onion-orchid

Microtis arenaria

J F M A M J J A S O N D

Flower size ≈ 0.4 cm   Plant height ≈ 60 cm

Common Ruddyhood

Oligochaetochilus squamatus

Synonym: *Pterostylis squamata*

J	F	M	A	M	J	J	A	S	O	N	D

Flower size ≈ 1.5 cm   Plant height ≈ 30 cm

Common Ruddyhood

Green form

Mantis Orchid

Arachnorchis tentaculata

Synonym: *Caladenia tentaculata*

J F M A M J J A S O N D

Flower size ≈ 10.0 cm   Plant height ≈ 50 cm

Salmon Sun-orchid

Thelymitra rubra

J F M A M J J A **S** O N D

Flower size ≈ 2.5 cm   Plant height ≈ 40 cm

Hooded Caladenia

Stegostyla cucullata

Synonym: *Caladenia cucullata*

J F M A M J J A **S** **O** **N** D

Flower size ≈ 2.0 cm   Plant height ≈ 35 cm

Common Onion-orchid

Microtis unifolia

J F M A M J J A S **O** **N** D

Flower size ≈ 0.4 cm   Plant height ≈ 90 cm

Spotted Sun-orchid

Summer

Only the hardiest are now in bloom.
Look out for snakes, flies and bushfires
and take plenty of drinking water with you.

Large Tongue Orchid

Rosy Hyacinth-orchid

Dipodium roseum

J	F	M	A	M	J	J	A	S	O	N	D

Flower size ≈ 2.5 cm   Plant height ≈ 100 cm

Rosy Hyacinth-orchid

Green stemmed

Large Tongue Orchid

Cryptostylis subulata

Flower size ≈ 3.0 cm   Plant height ≈ 80 cm

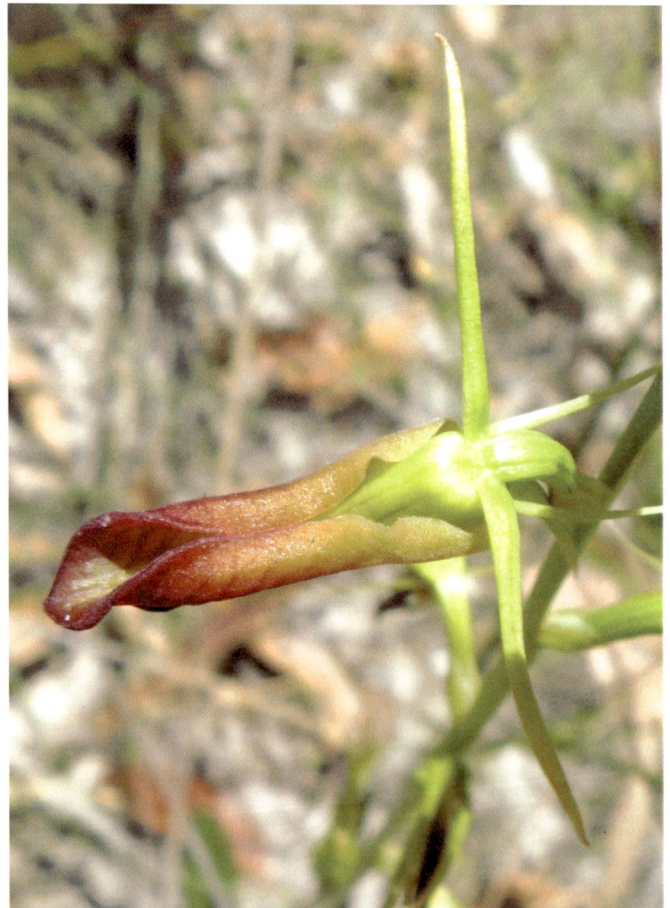

Purple Hyacinth-orchid

Dipodium punctatum

| J | F | M | A | M | J | J | A | S | O | N | D |

Flower size ≈ 2.0 cm   Plant height ≈ 800 cm

Slender Beard-orchid

Calochilus therophilus

J **F** M A M J J A S O N **D**

Flower size ≈ 3.0 cm   Plant height ≈ 70 cm

Sharp Midge Orchid

Corunastylis despectans

Flower size ≈ 0.4 cm   Plant height ≈ 30 cm

Rosy Hyacinth-orchid

Autumn

When will the autumn rains arrive?
Some orchids are just waiting for the
moisture to flower before the cold sets in.

Large Autumn Greenhood

Tiny Greenhood

Speculantha parviflora

Synonym: *Pterostylis parviflora*

J F **M A M J** J A S O N D

Flower size ≈ 1.0 cm   Plant height ≈ 25 cm

Parson's Bands

Eriochilus cucullatus

J F **M A M** J J A S O N D

Flower size ≈ 2.0 cm   Plant height ≈ 25 cm

Large Autumn Greenhood

Diplodium revolutum

Synonym: *Pterostylis revoluta*

| J | F | M | A | M | J | J | A | S | O | N | D |

Flower size ≈ 4.5 cm   Plant height ≈ 25 cm

Slaty Helmet Orchid

Corysanthes incurva

Synonym: *Corybas incurvus*

J F M A **M J J A S** O N D

Flower size ≈ 1.5 cm   Plant height ≈ 1.5 cm

Small Mosquito Orchid

Acianthus pusillus

J F M **A M J J A** S O N D

Flower size ≈ 0.5 cm   Plant height ≈ 18 cm

Small Mosquito Orchid

Green form

Striped Greenhood

Diplodium striatum

Synonym: *Pterostylis striata*

J F M **A M J J A** S O N D

Flower size ≈ 3.0 cm   Plant height ≈ 25 cm

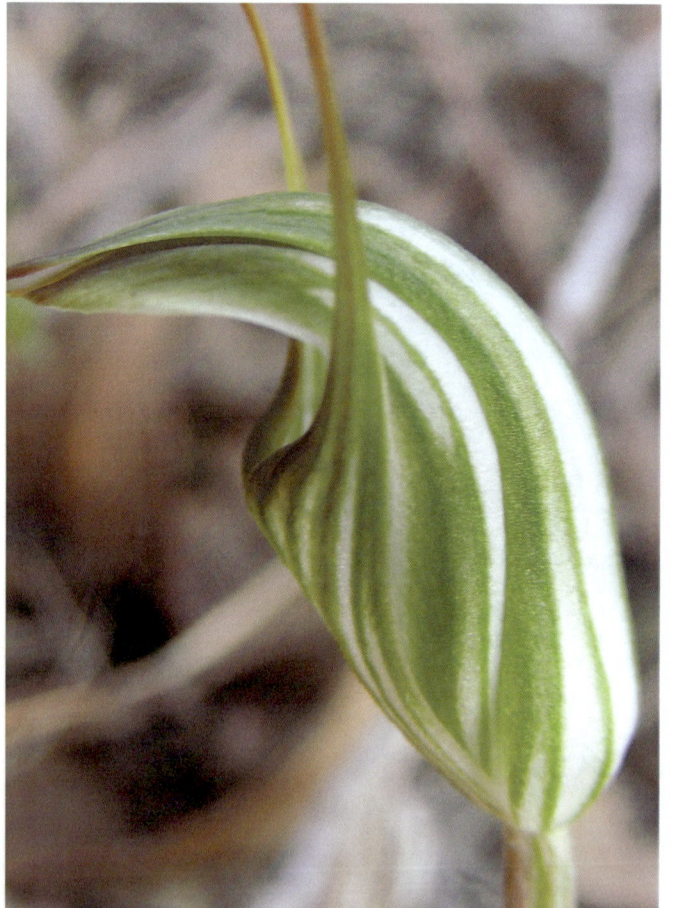

Winter

Cold loving orchids and those getting a head start on spring are out now. Make sure you have rain protection for both you and your camera.

Wine-lip Spider-orchid

Trim Greenhood

Pterostylis concinna

J F M A **M** **J** **J** **A** **S** O N D

Flower size ≈ 1.5 cm   Plant height ≈ 20 cm

Gnat Orchid

Cyrtostylis reniformis

J F M A M J **J A S O** N D

Flower size ≈ 3.5 cm   Plant height ≈ 16 cm

Leafy (Tall) Greenhood

Bunochilus melagrammus

Synonym: *Pterostylis melagramma*

J F M A **M J J A S** O N D

Flower size ≈ 1.5 cm   Plant height ≈ 80 cm

Leafy (Tall) Greenhood

Other forms

Nodding Greenhood

Pterostylis nutans

J F M A **M** J **J A S O** N D

Flower size ≈ 2.5 cm   Plant height ≈ 30 cm

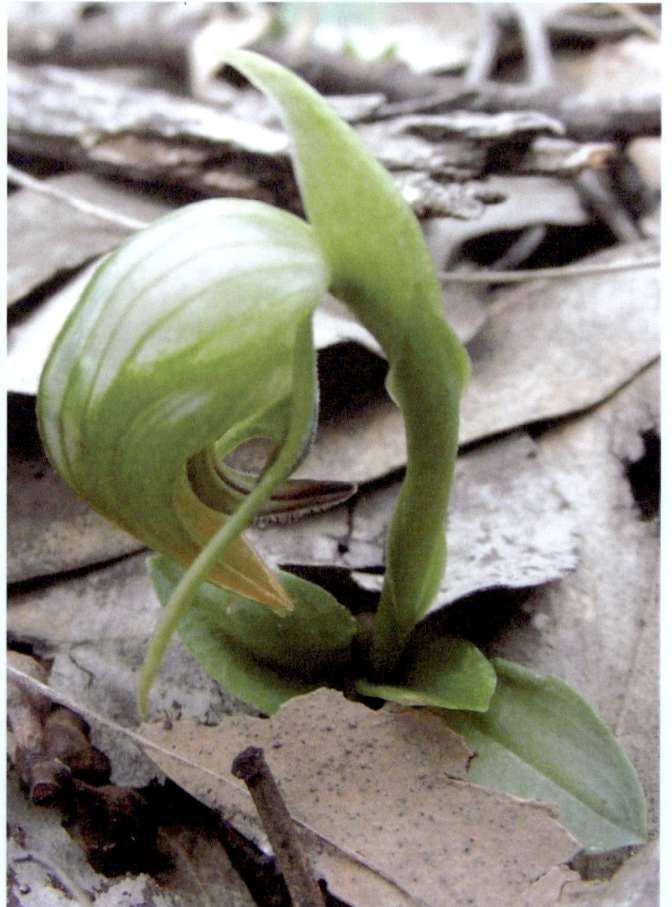

Dwarf Greenhood

Linguella nana

Synonym: *Pterostylis nana*

J F M A M J J A S O N D

Flower size ≈ 2.0 cm   Plant height ≈ 20 cm

Veined Helmet Orchid

Corysanthes diemenica

Synonym: *Corybas dilatatus*

J F M A M J J A S O N D

Flower size ≈ 1.5 cm   Plant height ≈ 1.5 cm

Emerald-lipped Greenhood

Bunochilus smaragdynus

Synonym: *Pterostylis smaragdyna*

J F M A M J J A S O N D

Flower size ≈ 1.5 cm   Plant height ≈ 80 cm

Early Caladenia

Stegostyla praecox

Synonym: *Caladenia praecox*

J F M A M J J **A S** O N D

Flower size ≈ 3.0 cm   Plant height ≈ 15 cm

Bearded Greenhood

Plumatichilos plumosum

Synonym: *Pterostylis plumosa*

J F M A M J J **A S O** N D

Flower size ≈ 3.5 cm   Plant height ≈ 25 cm

Wine-lip Spider-orchid

Arachnorchis oenochila

Synonym: *Caladenia oenochila*

J F M A M J J A S O N D

Flower size ≈ 8.0 cm   Plant height ≈ 30 cm

Wine-lip Spider-orchid

Variations

Rosella Spider-orchid

Arachnorchis rosella

Synonym: *Caladenia rosella*

J F M A M J J A S O N D

Flower size ≈ 6.0 cm   Plant height ≈ 17 cm

Leopard Orchid

Diuris pardina

J F M A M J J A S O N D

Flower size ≈ 3.0 cm   Plant height ≈ 30 cm

Maroonhood

Pterostylis pedunculata

J F M A M J J A S O N D

Flower size ≈ 2.0 cm   Plant height ≈ 25 cm

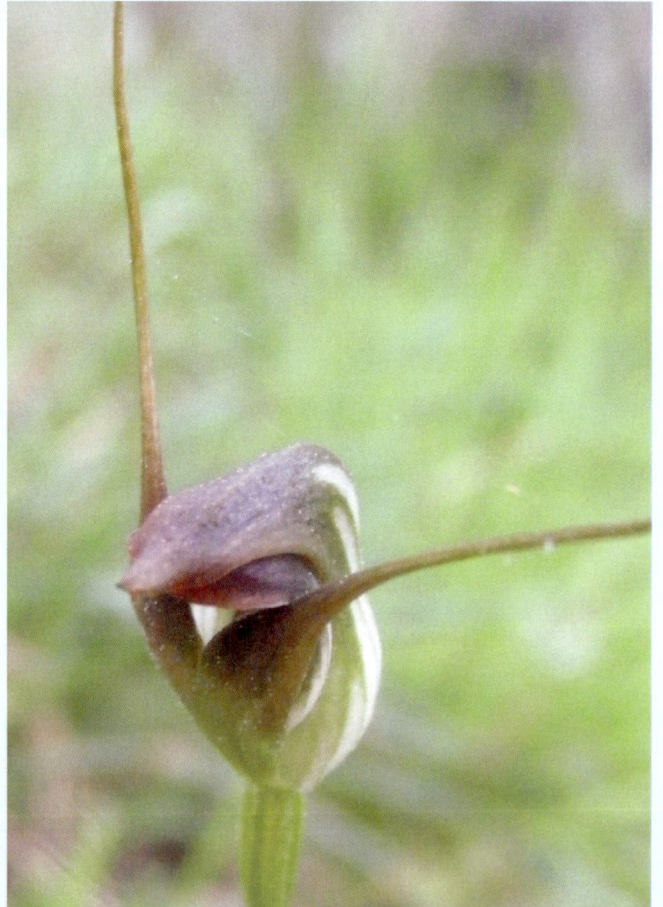

Maroonhood

Colour variations

Blunt Greenhood

Pterostylis curta

J F M A M J J A S O N D

Flower size ≈ 3.5 cm   Plant height ≈ 30 cm

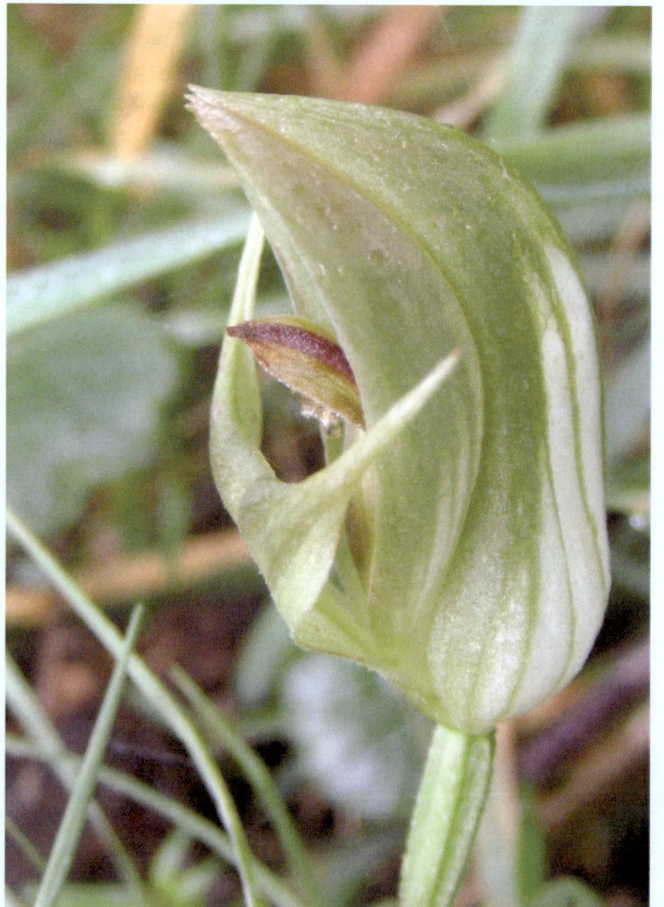

Mayfly Orchid

Nemacianthus caudatus

Synonym: *Acianthus caudatus*

J F M A M J J A S O N D

Flower size ≈ 4.5 cm   Plant height ≈ 14 cm

Blue Caladenia

Cyanicula caerulea

Synonym: *Caladenia caerulea*

J F M A M J J A S O N D

Flower size ≈ 2.5 cm   Plant height ≈ 15 cm

Blue Caladenia

Pale form

Leopard Orch